How To Teach the Paragraph

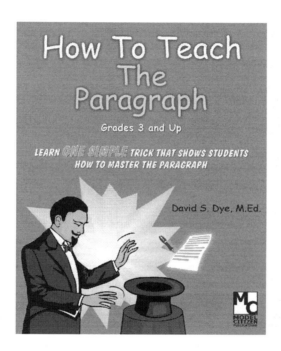

From David Dye's Writing Workshop:
The Complete Writing Program

Staff Development information is
available at CreateBetterWriters.com

Copyright © 2005 / 2012 Model Citizen Publications, David S. Dye

Introduction

In my writing workshops I present this lesson to show teachers how to teach the paragraph. I've run into teachers who have taken my workshop years in the past who continue to praise this technique. It's quick, powerful, and effective. Best of all, if you are using *The Complete Writing Program* (available at CreateBetterWriters.com), the quick learners move on to bigger and better things, leaving you time to reinforce this essential skill with the rest of your class.

Notice that I referred to paragraph writing as an essential skill. You may have already known that by instinct, but make it the dominant thought on your mind as you teach writing. The paragraph is the foundation of great writing. If a student can write an intelligent, well-organized paragraph, they are well on their way to great writing.

Overview

Here I will review the steps. At times, two or three steps can be done in a day. Follow each step at your class's pace. Take your time if you must; this is a crucial skill. After the overview, I will explain the steps in greater detail.

Paragraph Writing – Overview

Part I – The Basics

Step 1 – Assessment: Students write a paragraph   (p. 2)

Step 2 – Learning the five parts of a good paragraph   (p. 3)

Step 3 – Memorize the Five Parts of a Paragraph   (p. 3)

Step 4 – The Paper Set-Up   (p. 4)

Step 5 – Write a Paragraph Together: The Prewrite   (p. 6)

Step 6 – Write a Paragraph Together: The Paragraph   (p. 7)

Part II – Improving the Parts of a Paragraph

Step 7 – Topic Sentences   (p. 9)

Step 8 – Closing Sentences   (p. 11)

Step 9 – Paragraph Assessment   (p. 13)

Step 10 – Practice, Practice, Practice   (p. 13)

Step 11 – The Perfect Paragraph   (p. 15)

Appendix A   (p. 17)   /   Appendix B   (p. 20)

Part I – The Basics

Step 1 – Assessment: Students Write a Paragraph.

I've taught third through eighth grade, and every year I begin with the paragraph. With this system, if a student can write a good paragraph, they will be able to write anything from stories to essays to research reports. In the next few steps you will learn one simple trick that will make paragraph writing incredibly easy. If you continue with *How To Teach the Five Paragraph Essay* and *The Complete Writing Program*, you will see how easy it is for you students to transition almost effortlessly to the essay, story writing and much more.

On the first day of school, ask students to write a paragraph about something that they did over the summer. This is a nice, broad topic and allows you to spot key mistakes right away. Will the students write about several different activities or just one? Will they stick to one main idea? How many sentences will they write? The only help I give them is to say that I am checking to see if they know how to write a paragraph. "What ever you think a good paragraph should be, show me!" is all I say.

You may want to repeat the process on the second day. Maybe they were rusty from the long summer break. You can have them write another paragraph about something else that they did over the summer.

Finally, take the students' second paragraphs, read them, and make a list. Check off how many students had a topic sentence, closing sentence, at least four supporting details, and stuck to one main idea. You will use this information later to show them how close (or far) they are to writing strong paragraphs.

Step 1 Summary:
A. Give a paragraph pretest.
B. Make a checklist: Do the students know how to write a topic / closing sentence?
   Do the students use supporting details?
   Do the students stick to One Main Idea?

Step 2 – Learning the Five Parts: Let the students try to guess the five parts of a good paragraph.

Number 1 – 5 on the board. Have the students number 1-5 on their papers. Let the students try to guess the five parts of the paragraph. Make a game out of it. Offer five raffle tickets or a small prize to the student who can name the #1 part of a paragraph. (The list is in

> **A Good Paragraph**
> 1. One Main Idea
> 2. Topic Sentence
> 3. 5-7 Sentences
> 4. Closing Sentence
> 5. Indent; Spelling and Punctuation

order of importance.) Offer four raffle tickets for the student who guesses the second item and so on. As the students correctly name an item on the list, write it on the board in its proper sequence. If the students say "Topic Sentence", put it next to number two and repeat this for all five steps. The class will have fun, and it will get them thinking about everything they've ever been taught about writing. This is a great time of review, even if they don't discover all five. For the classes that aren't coming close, give as many hints as you can until they get it.

When finished, heavily emphasize that a paragraph is about ONE MAIN IDEA. Do call and response over and over: "What is a paragraph about?" The class will respond, "ONE MAIN IDEA". Look each student in the eyes and ask, "What is a paragraph about?" The student responds, "ONE MAIN IDEA". Ask them during math, on the way to lunch, and when you see them on the playground. It should become a reflex, like when a doctor taps your knee with that little hammer. A paragraph is about ONE MAIN IDEA!

Step 2 Summary:
A. Number 1 – 5 on the board.
B. Have the students number 1-5 on their papers.
C. Let the students try to guess the five parts of the paragraph.
D. As the students guess correctly, write the items on the board in the correct sequence.

Step 3 – Memorize the Five Parts of a Paragraph

First, ask the class, "Who can name one item on the list without looking?" Next ask, "Who can name two items without looking?" Keep going until someone can name all five. If you're giving out a prize of some kind (Jolly Ranchers, Raffle Tickets, etc.) the kids will be studying frantically while another student is answering.

In my workshop, I show teachers another trick that will help students memorize the parts of a paragraph. Basically, have the students draw a picture of the paragraph. Put an X where the paragraph should be indented. We'll draw a line with a period at the end to represent the topic sentence. The topic sentence tells the ONE MAIN IDEA. We'll draw five more lines with periods then write 5-7 on top of them to represent 5-7 sentences. Finally, we'll make a large circle for the last period and put a CS to represent the Closing Sentence.

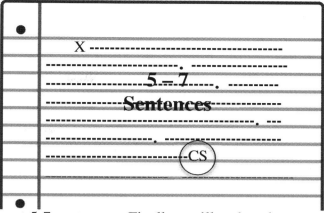

You can use either method or both. Whatever way you choose, give the students five minutes to practice saying the five parts of a paragraph as quickly as they can. Time them to see how fast they can say them. When a student really knows the five parts, they are able to say them in less than five seconds. You can make it a test by practicing daily and give them an official time at the end of the week.

Step 3 Summary:
   A. Have a student name one part of the paragraph. Next, have a student name two parts. Repeat until someone can name all five parts.
   B. Draw a picture of a paragraph. Use each piece of the picture to help memorize the parts of the paragraph.
   C. Give students five minutes to practice saying the five parts of a paragraph as quickly as they can.

Step 4 – The Paper Set-Up

This step is the one simple trick that will make writing the paragraph incredibly easy. You can use this trick to teach almost any type of writing. I use it to teach essay writing, research reports, stories, and more. Students can even use it as an outline for oral presentations. There is NO LIMIT on how far your students can take this. I've had former fifth graders, while in high school, come back and tell me that this trick saved them. They still remember it and use it regularly.

Tell your students about the magic words. The magic words are: "You are about to write a paragraph." Whenever they hear these magic words, they are to do the following immediately: (Model it for them on the board and have them copy as you complete each step)

A. Put your name and date at the top right hand corner of the paper.
B. Put "Prewrite" on the top line in the middle.
C. Write "One Main Idea:" on the first line of your paper with the number 1 below it.
D. Make a cluster in the middle of your paper, put your pencil down and wait for the topic. See Part I – Paper Set-Up below. (Many teachers despise the cluster. If you're one of them, feel free to have them number from 1 to 5 on their paper.)

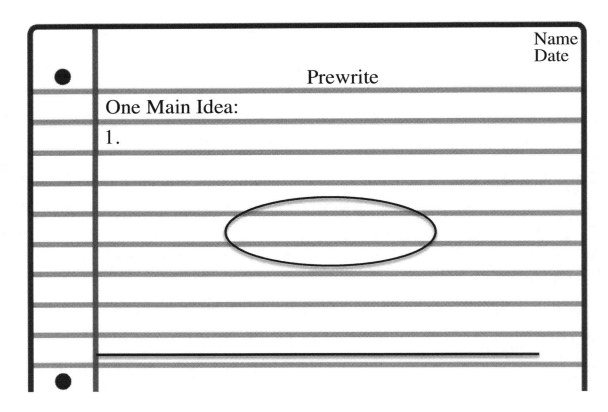

That's it! That is all there is to the one simple trick. You may be wondering how this will lead to easy paragraph writing. It will all become clear as we continue through the steps.

At this point, have the students turn their paper over. Ask them to write as much of the paper set-up as they can remember. Only let them look at the model after they have written as much as they can from memory. Have the students repeat this process over and over until they have completely memorized how to set up their paper for a paragraph.

Step 4 Summary:

See Steps A – D above.

CreateBetterWriters.com

Step 5 – Write a Paragraph Together: The Prewrite

When the students have shown that they understand how to set-up their papers, you can write a paragraph together. To keep it simple, write a paragraph about how to write a paragraph.

A. Give the topic "The Paragraph". Immediately, have the students write the topic above the word "Prewrite".

B. One Main Idea: In one sentence, have the students explain what the paragraph is about. Later, you will explain that they are actually writing the topic sentence. The sentence can be written in many ways. An example would be "Writing a paragraph is easy."

C. The students think of five details that will support that main idea. Obviously, they will write the five parts of a paragraph around the cluster. Show them that they do not need to write complete sentences here. Their main goal is just to get their ideas down on paper.

D. Finally, have them number the items in the cluster. Put them in the order that they will appear in the paragraph. This will help the paragraph have a smooth flow.

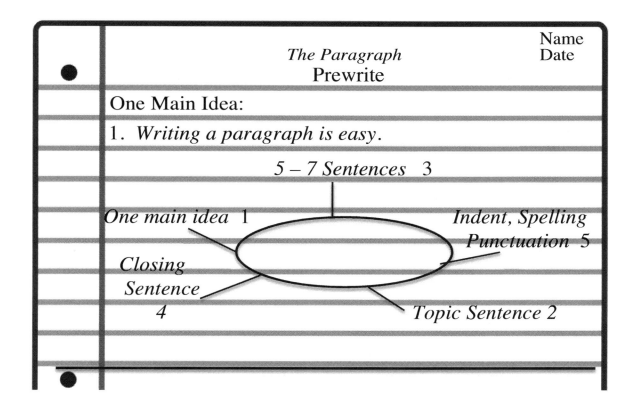

Step 5 Summary:

See Steps A – D above.

CreateBetterWriters.com

Step 6 – Write a Paragraph Together: The Paragraph

The hardest part is now over. If your students can produce a good prewrite, the actual writing is incredibly easy. The prewrite shows them what to do. As you model this section, be sure to emphasize the connection between the prewrite and the paragraph.

A. Below the middle line in the middle of the paper, have them put an X about an inch from the red margin. This is where the paragraph will begin.

B. The Topic Sentence: Review the parts of a paragraph. **Ask** your students again, "What is a paragraph about?" **Answer**: One Main Idea. **Ask**: What sentence tells the One Main Idea? **Answer**: The Topic Sentence.

Have the students point to the one main idea on their prewriting. Point out that we have already written the one main idea. Would this make a good topic sentence? Absolutely! Thus, we've already written the first sentence of our paragraph.

For the older students, ask them about the quality of the topic sentence. "Writing a paragraph is easy." is a simple sentence worthy of third graders, not for older students. Have them improve the sentence by saying the same thing, only with more style. For example, the older students can write, "With only a few simple steps, anyone can write an outstanding paragraph." The idea is the same. The only difference is that the quality is improved.

C. Supporting Details: Have the students write a sentence for each of the items in the cluster. Remind them that the items are numbered. What is great about this system is that the students are now able to focus on **how** to phrase their sentences rather that **what** to say in their sentences. If you are using CreateBetterWriters.com's *Writing Tricks Plus*, the students would now be thinking about intelligent ways to write these sentences rather than writing boring, simple sentences.

D. Closing Sentence: Think of the closing sentence as the bow on the package. Whenever a gift is wrapped, the bow adds that nice final touch. The closing sentence does this for the paragraph.

CreateBetterWriters.com

The closing sentence can serve three purposes. First, it can summarize the one main idea. Since you've already written the one main idea, you can simply restate it at the end such as "If you know these simple steps, you will have no problem writing a paragraph." Second, it can give final thoughts or opinions about the topic. An example would be "Following these steps is a good way to keep your writing organized." Finally, it can serve as a transition to the next paragraph's main idea. If your next paragraph is about how to write an essay, your closing sentence could be "You can follow these simple steps to master many other types of writing."

Step 6 Summary:

A. Have the students put an X where they will begin their paragraph.
B. Write the Topic Sentence together. Point out that the One Main Idea from the prewriting can be used to write a good topic sentence.
C. Write the Supporting Details together. Show how they can use the numbered items in the cluster to write an organized paragraph. This is also a good time to show students how to create margins by staying between the red lines of the paper.
D. Write a Closing Sentence together. Use the One Main Idea again to summarize, give final thoughts, or transition to the next paragraph.

Part II – Improving the Paragraph

After teaching the paragraph for so long, I've discovered many subtle tricks to reinforce the writing of topic sentences, closing sentences, supporting sentences, and prewriting. I do it throughout the day with many other lessons so this section has become obsolete for me. However, I came across these tricks by doing the activities below.

Steps 7 and 8 will be most appropriate for grades three through five. The older students seem to catch on without them. Use the Steps 7 and 8 below if your students seem to need an extra push when completing the paragraph. It is definitely worth the time and trouble. Remember, once the students have mastered the paragraph, they have a strong foundation for all types of writing.

Step 7 – Topic Sentences

Any given topic can have thousands of main ideas. Suppose you ask your students to write about pizza. How many different main ideas could they come up with for this? 1. How to make a pizza; 2. Their favorite pizza place; 3. History of pizza; 4. Best times to each pizza; 5. Different kinds of pizza…

All of these main ideas would make good paragraphs. Teach the students to narrow their focus to one specific main idea. The flip side of this is that the students must be careful not to make their main idea so narrow that they cannot think of five to seven things to say about it. For example, if their topic is "pizza", and their main idea is "pepperoni", they may have a hard time writing five to seven sentences about pepperoni.

This is what they are going to do: Give the students several different <u>broad</u> topics. Have them come up with three main ideas for each. Each of these main ideas should be something specific about that topic that they can think of five to seven details about it. If they cannot think of five to seven details, this means that their main idea is too narrow. Three good topics for this assignment are Pizza, Ice Cream, and Friends. The following shows how you can have your students set up their papers:

Students can format their papers for this assignment like this:

```
                    Topic Sentences
Pizza:
1.
2.
3.

Ice Cream:
1.
2.
3.

Friends:
1.
2.
3.
```

As a Class:
Come up with suggestions for pizza together. Make a list on the board and have the students select good main ideas. This will give you a good opportunity to discuss the quality of the main ideas with your students. If someone suggests, "cheesy", you might ask, "Can you think of five to seven things to say about 'cheesy'?" You might recommend "Why

CreateBetterWriters.com

pizza tastes so good". When finished, you might have ideas such as: How to make a pizza, Restaurants with the best pizza, Different kinds of crusts, History of pizza, Family Pizza Night, The best toppings for pizza. Ultimately, when finished, the students can select their favorite three.

Individually: When the students finish selecting their three main ideas, have them repeat the procedure for Ice Cream and Friends. They need to think of three main ideas that would make good paragraphs.

Group Share: When everyone is finished, have the students share their ideas. There is a space for a fourth main idea under each item. Allow them to write down one more main idea for each topic as they hear other students share their favorite main ideas.

Follow-up: You may consider repeating this lesson as many times as it takes until you feel that your students get the idea. This activity would make a great warm-up to the day. Simply put a topic on the board and have the students think of three main ideas that would make good paragraphs.

Writing Topic Sentences:
If you feel that your students catch on quickly, you might consider doing this step as you select your three main ideas. If not, repeat the Follow-up until the students have it mastered.
The basic idea is to have the students write a topic sentence for each of their main ideas. The students can set up their papers just as they did for the previous activity. This time, have them write a sentence that would introduce the topic.

The goal here is to get the students to tell the main idea of the paragraph. They may be tempted to add details to their topic sentence. This is a good time to put a stop to this. Again, you will write the topic sentences with them as you start with Pizza. Ask for volunteers to offer suggestions about good topic sentences. This will be a

	Topic Sentences
	Pizza:
	1. There are many great places to get good pizza.
	2.
	3.
	Ice Cream:
	1.

good time to offer suggestions about what makes a good topic sentence. A student might suggest, "There are many great places to get great pizza like Checkers, Little Neros, and Joe's Pizza." This would be a good opportunity to show the students that the places to get the pizza will go in the body of the paragraph. They should just stick to the main idea "There are many great places to get pizza."

> **Step 7 Summary:**
> A. Give the students broad topics such as Pizza, Ice Cream, and Friends.
>   1. Select three main ideas for the first (Pizza). Discuss whether the main idea is too narrow or just right.
>   2. All the students to finish the other topics on their own. Have the students share their ideas and add their favorites to their own paper.
>   3. Review this procedure daily if more practice is needed.
> B. Have the students write topic sentences for each of their main ideas. Write the first three together then allow them to finish on their own. When finished, have the students share their sentences and discuss the quality. Again, do this as a daily journal activity if more practice is needed.

Step 8 – Closing Sentences (and Topic Sentences)

To review, the closing sentence either summarizes the one main idea, gives final thoughts or opinions, or forms a transition to the next paragraph. The danger with the closing sentence is that it can come across as clumsy. This is fine for the young writer. They will become more polished as they get older.

This step is very similar to Step 7. Give the students some very broad topics. The students will:
1. List three main ideas that would make good paragraphs.
2. Write three topic sentences for each main idea.
3. Write three closing sentences for each main idea.

*Note: See the illustration on the next page. A worksheet for this step is provided in the appendix.

Since the students will not be writing the body of these paragraphs, you will need them to imagine that they've written the paragraphs as they think of good closing sentences. After modeling it a few times, the students should get the hang of it.

Topic Sentences

Parties:

Main Idea #1

Topic Sentence #1

Closing Sentence #1

Main Idea #2

Topic Sentence #2

Closing Sentence #2

Main Idea #3

Topic Sentence #3

Closing Sentence #3

Students can use the worksheets in the appendix to complete this task. The first worksheet has the topic "Parties" ready for them. They will think of a main idea for parties, write a topic sentence for that main idea, and finally create a closing sentence. They will then repeat the process for a second and third main idea.

The second worksheet leaves the topic blank. Have them repeat this step for topics such as Hobbies and Best Way to Spend a Day. If they need more practice, select topics that interest them. You can copy this worksheet as many times as you need until the students have the closing sentence mastered.

Step 8 Summary:

A. Give the students broad topics such as Parties, Hobbies, and Best Way to Spend a Day.

B. For each topic, have the students think of three main ideas. Have them list them under each of the main ideas on their papers.

C. Have the students write a topic sentence for each of the main ideas.

D. Finally, have them write closing sentences for each of the main ideas.

E. If more practice is needed, do one topic a day as a review.

Step 9 – Paragraph Assessment
Students check each other for five parts of the paragraph.

From now on, whenever the students write paragraphs, have them check each other for the five parts of a good paragraph. They can use this worksheet (located at the end of this document) to give each other a score. By checking each other's writing for the five parts of the paragraph, they are reinforcing the five parts for themselves and seeing other paragraphs modeled by other students.

```
Paragraph Assessment
1. This paragraph has a topic sentence:
        1     2     3     4
2. This paragraph has 5 to 7 sentences:
        1     2     3     4
3. This paragraph has a closing sentence:
        1     2     3     4
4. The paragraph sticks to one main idea:
        1     2     3     4
5. The paragraph is indented:
        1     2     3     4
```

When they score, a four indicates that the step was done very well. A three is passing, but it could have been better. A two and one would tell the writer that they could have done much better. Have the students use this scoring sheet to conference with each other. Allow the students to explain why they gave their scores. You might hear students repeating your lessons from the previous steps. Your words become more powerful when they come from your students to each other.

Step 9 Summary:
A. Have students trade their paragraphs and check for each part of the paragraph. A score of a three or four indicates mastery.
B. Have the students explain their scores to each other. This will reinforce the lesson you have taught.

Step 10 – Practice, Practice, Practice
This is what your students have learned:
A. When they hear the magic words, "You're about to write a paragraph," the student know how to set up their papers.
B. You give them the topic. They will write the topic at the top, narrow the topic by writing their one main idea, list five to seven details about the main idea, and number them in the correct order.
C. Write the paragraph.

Depending on the age of the student, it can take between a day and a month to master these steps. Once mastery is achieved, the students have a technique that will make all types of writing incredibly easy.

Give the students plenty of practice until complete mastery is achieved. Do several paragraphs with them until they are confident enough to do it on their own. It will be well worth the time.

Here are some suggestions for paragraphs:

Language Arts:
1. Summarize stories.
2. Describe your favorite character or scene from the story.
3. What character in the story is most/least like you?
4. After reading a story, write a one-paragraph sequel. What would happen next if the story continued?
5. Write a one-paragraph story. Make sure it has a beginning, middle, and end.
    Here are some topics:
    - The Thing Under My Bed!
    - A Fun day with a Friend
    - The Piñata
    - The Silly Cat
    - How I lost My Tooth.
    - The Monkey Escape!
    - Describe a real life day at the beach, on a plane, at a park, at sporting event, or another location you want to write about.

Math:
1. Objects in the world shaped like circles / squares / quadrilaterals.
2. Explain how to do a certain procedure such as borrowing or dividing.
3. Write a one-paragraph word problem.
4. Explain the Order of Operations procedure.

Social Studies / Science / Health:
1. Describe how a caterpillar turns into a butterfly.
2. Explain a day in the life of the Tlingit tribe.
3. Write a summary of a major event.
4. Summarize an experiment.
5. Write a biography about an important historical figure.
6. Create an emergency plan to help your family prepare for any natural disaster that might occur.

The possibilities are endless. When your students begin to master the paragraph, it will only take about ten minutes to prewrite and write the paragraph. Considering how good writing is at reinforcing learning, a ten minute summary is a small investment that offers big returns.

Step 10 Summary
  A. Practice, Practice, Practice. Make sure students are using the paper set-up correctly. Give topic after topic until the students can write a paragraph completely on their own without any help from you. Besides practicing the paragraph, it is a great way to reinforce the other subjects you are teaching.
  B. Check out *How To Teach the Five Paragraph Essay*. Once the students can write the paragraph, writing essays is just a few more steps away. Use the same technique to write strong essays with excellent introductions and conclusions.

Step 11 – The Perfect Paragraph
Try this activity to get students writing strong paragraphs with good spelling and punctuation. When your students get lazy with the quality of their sentences and their grammar, this is a great way to keep them sharp. They will stay sharp for a long time knowing that this lesson is a possibility if the quality of their paragraphs begins to slip.

In this step, the students must write the perfect paragraph. Any little mistake will result in them having to rewrite the entire paragraph.
  A. Give them a topic. Students prewrite and write the paragraph. Collect the paragraphs and look for any flaw you can find.
  B. Return the paragraphs. The students must rewrite their paragraphs and bring them to you when finished. Note, a line may start to form at your desk as many students finish at the same time. Only allow three to wait in line. Have them work on another assignment, such as a book report, if they need to wait.
  C. Give the students five tries to complete the perfect paragraph. If the students complete it in the first three tries, give them an A. On the fourth try, they can receive a B. On the fifth try, they get a C. The students who don't complete the perfect paragraph get to write a second paragraph. If the paragraph has all the required parts such as a topic sentence, supporting details, and a closing sentence, give them a C as well.

Conclusion:

Depending on the age of the students, you may need to model the prewriting and writing of the paragraphs several times. The average fifth grader may need to see it done several times before being able to do it alone. After a month of practice, they can summarize stories from their literature books, explain science lessons, or describe a field trip in about ten minutes. They get so good at writing paragraphs, it becomes second nature. Be sure to give them many opportunities to use this skill.

High school students can learn the procedure in a day. After teaching the paragraph, give them five terms from a vocabulary list to summarize. Have them prewrite and write the paragraphs for practice. If you are using this with older students, you are probably using this lesson plan to prepare them for the five-paragraph essay. Writing the summaries will help prepare them for this.

The fantastic aspect of this method is that learning other forms of writing is so easy. They will follow the same steps for the paragraph to transition to all kinds of writing such as the essay, story writing, research reports and much more. For more information about how this works, you can find *How To Teach the Five Paragraph Essay* at CreateBetterWriters.com.

Appendix A
Topic Sentence Worksheets

Name: _____

Topic Sentences

Topic: Parties

Main Idea #1:

_____

Topic Sentence #1:

_____

Closing Sentence #1:

_____

Main Idea #2:

_____

Topic Sentence #2:

_____

Closing Sentence #2:

_____

Main Idea #3:

_____

Topic Sentence #3:

_____

Closing Sentence #3:

_____

Name: _____

Topic Sentences

Topic: _____

Main Idea #1:

_____

Topic Sentence #1:

_____

Closing Sentence #1:

_____

Main Idea #2:

_____

Topic Sentence #2:

_____

Closing Sentence #2:

_____

Main Idea #3:

_____

Topic Sentence #3:

_____

Closing Sentence #3:

_____

Appendix B
Paragraph Assessment
Worksheet

Author's Name: _____
Editor's Name: _____

Paragraph Assessment

1. This paragraph has a topic sentence:

          1   2   3   4

2. This paragraph has 5 to 7 sentences:

          1   2   3   4

3. This paragraph has a closing sentence:

          1   2   3   4

4. The paragraph sticks to one main idea:

          1   2   3   4

5. The paragraph is indented:

          1   2   3   4

Author's Name: _____
Editor's Name: _____

Paragraph Assessment

1. This paragraph has a topic sentence:

          1   2   3   4

2. This paragraph has 5 to 7 sentences:

          1   2   3   4

3. This paragraph has a closing sentence:

          1   2   3   4

4. The paragraph sticks to one main idea:

          1   2   3   4

5. The paragraph is indented:

          1   2   3   4

CreateBetterWriters.com

Made in the USA
San Bernardino, CA
14 May 2016